Burne-Jones
*An illustrated life of
Sir Edward Burne-Jones*

1833 - 1898
William Waters

Shire Publications Ltd.

Contents

ACKNOWLEDGEMENTS

The author and publishers wish to thank the following for permission to reproduce the illustrations on the pages indicated: Norham House Gallery, Cockermouth 2; Fitzwilliam Museum, Cambridge 14; William Morris Gallery 17·(lower and upper); Ashmolean Museum, Oxford 18; T. Hancock 21; Stone Gallery, Newcastle-upon-Tyne 22; T.W. Rowe 27 (upper); The Warden and Council of Bradfield College 27 (lower); Carlisle Art Gallery 29; Birmingham Art Gallery 30; Laing Art Gallery, Newcastle-upon-Tyne 31; City of Southampton Art Gallery 34; British Museum 36, 37; Mrs C. Wood 39; Piccadilly Gallery 40; Bradford City Art Gallery 41; Courtauld Institute of Art 43 (top right); Fred Hollyer 45. The illustration on page 4 is taken from 'Memorials of Edward Burne-Jones' by Georgiana Burne-Jones, that on page 11 from 'George Frederic Watts' by M. S. Watts, and that on page 9 from a private collection. The cover illustration is a detail from 'Laus Veneris', reproduced in full on page 31, by courtesy of Tyne and Wear Museums Service.

Printed by C. I. Thomas and Sons (Haverfordwest) Ltd, Press Buildings, Merlins Bridge, Haverfordwest, Dyfed.

Opposite: a pencil sketch of Burne-Jones made when he was in early middle age, by George Howard.

No.11 Bennett's Hill, Birmingham, where Burne-Jones was born. His father kept a carver and gilder's shop and the family lived above. The house has now been pulled down.

School life and Oxford

LIFE WITH FATHER

Birmingham, where Burne-Jones was born, was a city of very marked contrasts, especially in the period of his youth. For although, unlike Manchester or Leeds, there was but a small amount of heavy industry, it had the problem of a large underprivileged working class that was crowded into a small metropolitan area. Bennett's Hill, the road in which Burne-Jones lived, was respectable and middle-class but a short distance away was the squalor typical of English cities which had been subjected to years of expanding industrialisation. It was contact with these urban problems that partly decided the path which Burne-Jones's art was to follow. Unlike his friend of later years, William Morris, who attacked the evil, Burne-Jones reacted to this contact, which intensified the visionary power of his mind, by withdrawing into his inner world of fantasy.

Edward Coley Burne Jones (the hyphen was added much later), was born on 28th August 1833. Through a complication associated with the birth, his mother died the same week. His father, severely shaken by his wife's untimely death, blamed the child and had little to do with him, hiring one incompetent nurse after another to look after the boy. At last a more reliable one was found who became part of the family and stayed for many years. She and his father brought the child up as best they could, but as he developed Edward began to realise how distant were their true interests from his own. His father was a carver, framer and gilder and conducted his business at 11 Bennett's Hill, which gave his young son an awareness of pictures. In later life the artist recalled his father in this way:

'. . .a very poetical little fellow (the term 'little' he reserved for social inferiors or people of little consequence) very tender hearted and touching—quite unfit for the world into which he was pitched . . . he used to read me little poems he had made

5

himself—but as the time went he grew shy of reading them to me . . . he knew nothing at all of art and couldn't understand what it was all about or why it should be . . . but he had so much poetry in his nature as to unfit him for this world, poor little fellow!'

Likewise, his lack of communication with his nurse, Miss Sampson, is shown by his answer 'elephants' to her enquiry regarding his thoughts. Already, as a child, that individual journey of self discovery, inseparable from his art, had taken a characteristic mould and he was later able to explain 'I was always drawing, unmothered with a sad papa, without sister or brother, always alone, I was never unhappy, because I was always drawing.'

In 1844, when he was 11, he started to attend King Edward's School, Birmingham, which was a short walk away in New Street. The school building (now sadly pulled down) was the first combined effort of the two architects Sir Charles Barry and A.W.N. Pugin and was of some architectural merit which doubtless appealed to the youth's romanticism. At King Edward's he made important friendships that helped to develop his intellect and was more popular than would have been expected owing to his sense of humour and his ability to caricature the masters. He became intimate friends with Cormell Price and together they read the romantic literature available, including Macpherson's *Ossian* and Burger's *Leonore*. Gradually the circle of his friends increased as it was joined by Richard Watson Dixon, the future poet, Wilfred Heeley, and Henry Macdonald, all of whom he continued friendship with at university.

As the intellect grew so Burne-Jones's aesthetic sensibilities expanded. Each summer he migrated to relatives who lived in Leicestershire and during one of these periods he visited the Cistercian monastery in Charnwood Forest. The impression it made on him was deep; he was always of a religious turn of mind and the monks appealed to him, embodying a pious devotion to a mystic ideal. Pugin's architecture was a reincarnation of the medieval spirit that he sought in his dreams. Whilst staying at Hereford he met the Rev. John Goss and through him encountered the High Church Movement and the writings of Cardinal Newman. Newman became one of the inspiring forces in his life. 'In an age of sofas and cushions he

Edward Jones aged about 25, from a contemporary photograph in the possession of the artist's family, and only recently discovered.

taught me to be indifferent to comfort; and in an age of materialism he taught me to venture all on the unseen . . .'

The religion the cardinal taught had just the right emphasis on the spiritual mysteries of Christianity; he transformed the ritual into something wonderfully magical that was bound to appeal to the artist in Burne-Jones. Under this influence he determined to enter the Church.

Meanwhile, back in Birmingham he was attending the government school of design three evenings a week. His interests were widening; together with Cormell Price he began writing a history of the world, and when visiting London he spent long hours studying ancient sculpture and wandering through the botany and zoology galleries of the British Museum. Throughout his life friends remarked at the breadth of his learning and intellectual powers. As his years at school drew to an end it was decided that he should go up to Exeter College, Oxford, to study for the Church. It so happened that a boy from Marlborough College had chosen the same college at Oxford and from their first meeting they became fast friends; that boy was William Morris.

OXFORD

The rest of the men from King Edward's—Fulford, Dixon and Faulkner—were attending Pembroke College and it was here that Burne-Jones and Morris joined them. Initially Burne-Jones was enthusiastic about Oxford, such a contrast from grimy Birmingham, but this became modified by the contact he made with fellow students and the dons. They had none of his high ideals or his interest in the arts and so the group from Birmingham, under the leadership of Morris and Burne-Jones, began studying on their own. Dixon noticed that their bond was 'poetry and indefinite artistic and literary aspirations' and they read Tennyson, Edgar Allan Poe, Le Motte Fouqué, Charlotte M. Yonge, Hurrell Froude, Dickens, Carlyle, Kingsley and Ruskin.

Thrown in upon themselves through the unsympathetic views of their fellows, the group's ties became stronger. Their reading and activities were centred upon the Gothic Revival or the Oxford Movement. Morris collected Arundel prints and brass rubbings which he and Burne-Jones had made on their journeys around Oxford. He began writing poetry of a distinctly medieval turn. Burne-Jones initiated the idea that they should form a celibate society working in the poorer parts of London, very much following the influence of Hurrell Froude and Cardinal Newman. But gradually the orientation became more secular, and instead of focusing their attention upon the acts of the devil they began to attack ugliness. In a letter to his friend Price, still at King Edward's, Burne-Jones says,'. . .for we must enlist you, dear brother, in this crusade and Holy Warfare against the age, the heartless coldness of the time'.

The brotherhood which he was forming was to be known as The Order of Sir Galahad, and the group planned a magazine to voice its opinions. At first it was to have been a picture book with drawings by Burne-Jones, thus enabling the less literate population access to their ideas, but as they became more concerned with art than religion so the projected magazine became more intellectual. Financing the scheme was no problem because of the wealth available to Morris. Morris was to have been editor but relinquished the post. The magazine

An illustration by Burne-Jones to 'The Fairy Family', a collection of fairy tales of Europe retold by Archibald Maclaren, a fencing instructor and friend of Burne-Jones when he was at Oxford. First commissioned in 1854, the intention had been to have many illustrations and decorations but when the volume was published in 1857 it contained only two illustrations and a tailpiece. Many designs were made but the artist had developed so rapidly that he became ashamed of them and refused to give permission to reproduce them.

began enthusiastically enough but during the year when it appeared (1856) the group was fragmenting and this closed it after the twelfth issue. Burne-Jones contributed two atmospherically rich but rather naive tales, 'The Cousins' and 'A Northern Tale', and an essay on Thackeray's *The Newcomes* in which he declares his admiration for Ruskin, Holman Hunt, Richard Doyle and, most important, Rossetti. By 1856 Burne-Jones had encountered the Pre-Raphaelites through the writings of Ruskin and at the Royal Academy and in a collection at Oxford he had seen work by Madox Brown, Millais, Holman Hunt and Rossetti. 'I saw that the Pre-Raphaelites had indeed come at a time when there was need for them and resolved after my little ability to defend and claim a patient hearing from them.'

Inevitably, as a Gothicist Morris wanted to see at close hand the northern French cathedrals and so in 1854 he and

Burne-Jones set off with this in mind. This period of isolation, separated as they were from familiar surroundings, enabled them to see clearly the direction they wished to go; studying the architecture and drawing made them realise that neither wished to enter the Church. Finally, one evening on the quay at Le Havre they decided that they were meant for the arts and that Morris would study architecture and Burne-Jones would devote his life to painting.

Already Burne-Jones had received from a friend in Oxford, Archibald Maclaren, a commission for around 90 drawings for a book of fairy tales. The book *The Fairy Family* appeared later with only three drawings although Burne-Jones had completed about sixty. The designs use all the paraphernalia of contemporary romantic illustration, showing Burne-Jones to have borrowed from Richard Doyle, and even Turner, and the atmosphere he creates is a cross between Walter Scott, Charlotte M. Yonge and Fouquè. The later designs show the influence of the Pre-Raphaelites and Rossetti and it was because of this inconsistency that he felt unable to publish them.

During the Christmas vacation of 1855 Burne-Jones went up to London with the intention of meeting Rossetti. He had heard that Rossetti lectured at the Working Men's College—which was available to any member of the public. The artist came, and Burne-Jones so succumbed to his personality that he earnestly desired to talk with him. He was taken the following night to meet him and Rossetti invited him to his studio where they talked of the magazine and Morris's poetry. Burne-Jones did not reveal his ambition to be a painter. Rossetti wrote of Burne-Jones after this visit, '. . . one of the nicest young fellows in *Dreamland*'.

Although giving the impression of being shy, the young Burne-Jones was, in fact, able to keep his friends on the verge of hysterics with his stories and comic drawings. Just as he had overcome his timidity at school and won the admiration of his schoolmates with his talent for satirising the idiosyncrasies of the masters, he could cement friendships with his latent fun and good humour. But above all he impressed all he came across with his intense sense of commitment to art and his depth of intellect.

Clean shaven, he was not to grow the characteristic beard until a few years later; his appearance was boyish and he was much prone to hero-worship. Both he and Morris, at the time of leaving Oxford and meeting Rossetti, were prepared to sink their own interests, personalities even, when they encountered a sympathetic and mature point of view. Once they had adopted Rossetti as leader nothing else mattered; chapter and verse were taken from his book. A letter written describing a forthcoming visit to Little Holland House by the young artist reveals his attitude to his master. 'I am going with Rossetti to be introduced to a lot of swells who'll frighten me to death and make me keep close to his side all the time.' Of this visit Val Prinsep observed 'This time Rossetti was accompanied by a younger man who he declared was the greatest genius of the age—a shy, fair young man, with mild grey-blue eyes and straight light hair which was apt to straggle over his well-developed forehead—who spoke in an earnest impressive manner when he did speak—which was not often . . . he was almost painfully shy . . .'

ROSSETTI

Morris stayed on at Oxford to take a degree but at the same time joined the office of George Edmund Street, a Gothic

Little Holland House, from an illustration by F.L. Griggs, where the Prinseps entertained their illustrious friends. Here, Burne-Jones first met G.F. Watts.

Adam delving, a detail from the stained glass window in Bradfield College, Berkshire, 1857. The figure of Adam is taken from Rossetti and that of Eve presumably from Elizabeth Siddal. One of three lights, this window was made by Powell's of Whitefriars and demonstrates how advanced was Burne-Jones in his approach to window design; there is no canopy and he creates a dynamic pattern of diagonals.

Revival architect of the first order. Also articled to Street was Philip Webb, who became one of Morris's closest friends and a partner of his firm. Burne-Jones moved to London without taking his degree and lived in Chelsea. He attended Leigh's and Gandish's drawing schools in an attempt to catch up lost time, drawing from the model, but spent much time with Rossetti. In August, Street moved office to London, Morris and Burne-Jones then took rooms together in Upper Gordon Street and later Rossetti found them his old lodgings in Red Lion Square.

Rossetti's method of tuition was most uncharacteristic for its day; the practice at the Academy was to isolate each discipline and to make the student proficient by endless practice at it. Thus they would spend months drawing from the 'antique' (a classical sculpture) in black and white and were not allowed to use colour in their first year. Imaginative composition was excluded until sufficient dexterity had been maintained. Rossetti on the other hand encouraged this from the first; what good was it to have skill if the artist had nothing to say? He insisted on creativity in his pupils, he gave them confidence to strike out on their own, no matter what their shortcomings. Under his influence Morris decided to give up architecture and Dixon began painting.

Of Burne-Jones's work at this time Rossetti was loud in his praise: 'marvels of finish and imaginative detail' he wrote to a fellow painter. Continuing in the style of *The Fairy Family* illustrations, Burne-Jones worked in pen and ink on a small scale. The subjects he chose were from medieval legends, many from Malory's *Morte d'Arthur*, a book he had discovered whilst at Oxford, independently of Rossetti. They reveal in their technique a deep knowledge of engraving, especially of that of Albrecht Dürer.

Rossetti's idea, that whatever the technique an artist had he could produce a work of art if his mind had vision, caused him to embark upon and coerce his young friends into a project in the debating hall at Oxford. While visiting his friend the architect Benjamin Woodward, who was building the hall, he suggested painting murals, an offer that was accepted. He enlisted Morris, Arthur Hughes, Val Prinsep, Burne-Jones, Hungerford Pollen and Spencer Stanhope. The theme was from the *Morte d'Arthur*. They had a riotous time together; they met Swinburne and Jane Burden, the future wife of Morris; but they had no experience of the mural art. As well as being unfinished the painting quickly faded until little could be seen. Burne-Jones's inability to handle figure painting on a large scale was very evident, but he was maturing fast.

Through the activity of Rossetti he received a commission from the Whitefriars Stained Glass Company (Powells) to make designs for windows. He produced a figure of Christ as the Good Shepherd which was an immediate success with all those who saw it. Then followed a series, the climax of which are the St. Frideswide windows in Christ Church Cathedral, Oxford, executed for Woodward in 1860, and the east window at Waltham Abbey also made in 1860 in connection with Burges's restoration of that building. Burne-Jones also worked in conjunction with William Butterfield at Topcliffe Church in Yorkshire. In these windows by Powells and the latter by Lavers and Barraud, Burne-Jones worked in a highly polychromatic idiom that was characteristic of the Gothic Revival; the figures and their treatment were reminiscent of medieval art. Later, in the glass he was to design for Morris, Marshall, Faulkner and Co. he reacted from this type to pioneer glass with lower toned colour and freer, more realistic drawing.

When Morris moved with Burne-Jones into Red Lion Square he designed heavy, medievally inspired furniture for their rooms. Upon their surface they and Rossetti painted suitable legendary scenes. Philip Webb designed a wardrobe/cabinet for Burne-Jones who painted an elaborate episode from Chaucer's Prioress's Tale on the front. It was completed in 1859 and he gave it to Morris as a wedding present in 1860.

'Musicians', a study for the murals at Red House, c.1860. The ambitious Morris had hoped to make his house notable for the numerous murals it was to have contained. These musicians are part of the scene 'The Wedding of Sire Degravaunt' which can be seen today in the house.

London and marriage

LITTLE HOLLAND HOUSE

Mr and Mrs Thoby Prinsep took the artist G.F. Watts under their wing in Italy; on returning to England later, an alliance was once again formed with the artist and he took up residence with them in Little Holland House in Kensington. Here Mrs Prinsep entertained a wide variety of society and intellectual friends—Tennyson, George Howard, Coutts Lindsay, Tom Hughes, and many others. Rossetti and his friends Ruskin and Holman Hunt paid visits there and he took Burne-Jones along in 1857. Burne-Jones was most impressed by the polished bohemianism and breadth of culture of the milieu. He became friends with Watts, who was prone to take satellite youngsters. Watts had a great respect for tradition in art; he had none of the virtual iconoclasm of Rossetti and so began an uneasy bi-polarity for the young artist. Either he could follow Rossetti and obtain technique through discovery and invention or he could systematically develop on the lines of the academic principles as recommended by Watts. Watts worshipped at the shrine of Italy and was steeped in its painting. Whilst being impressed by these ideas Burne-Jones was simultaneously made to feel inadequate. When, after an illness brought upon by Rossetti's irregular hours and eating habits, he was taken bodily by Mrs Prinsep back to Little Holland House, his future was decided. He became a willing student of Italian painting and began a progressive system of improving his technique. All this was much to the alarm of Rossetti and Morris who keenly sensed the redirection of his interests. Rossetti's influence had been too deeply rooted to have been lost altogether but it had certainly become modified. Finally, Burne-Jones had to see for himself and so, in 1859 and again in 1861, we find him visiting Italy. The trip in 1859 was with Faulkner and Val Prinsep who kept a watchful eye on him; he made copies from Mantegna,

Titian, Botticelli, Tintoretto, Agnolo Gaddi, Giotto, Orcagna
and Benozzo Gozzoli.

FOUNDATION OF 'THE FIRM'

Morris fell in love with Jane Burden at Oxford, they married
in 1859 and he commissioned Philip Webb to design a house for
him at Bexley in Kent. In furnishing the house he was made to
realise the difficulty of finding articles to his requirements.
Through discussions with his friends the idea emerged of
founding a firm which could fill the need for well-designed
furniture and decoration. Burne-Jones had experience with
furniture and stained glass, Webb with household items, and the
others were keen to try their hand. And so the firm of Morris,
Marshall, Faulkner and Co. was founded. Webb, Rossetti,
Madox Brown, Burne-Jones and Arthur Hughes were
co-founders. It began in 1861.

Burne-Jones immediately designed stained glass, tiles, panels
for a fountain in Durham and for furniture. However Gothic
was the form of the superficial decoration of the firm's
productions, its inauguration heralded a new direction. At first
their art was based upon medieval prototypes but gradually
through the 1860s this became reduced. Their glass became
more secular with emphasis on realism and less dependent on
religious stylisation. Figure work became the most important
part of a window; canopies were dispensed with. The colour of
the earlier Gothic Revival glass of the firms Clayton and Bell,
Heaton and Butler, or Lavers and Barraud was highly chromatic;
Morris and his friends reacted away from this into earth colours,
olives, blues, and greens with high points in red. With Powell
and Company they were forging a new style which was to
become known in the 1870s as the Aesthetic Movement.

Burne-Jones's painting inevitably became influenced by his
activities in the decorative fields. *Green Summer, Backgammon
Players* and an early version of *King Cophetua* were firstly
decorations for cabinets designed by Philip Webb. The idea of
The Passing of Venus and *The Briar Rose* series first appeared in
tile form.

FRIENDS DURING THE 1860S

Rossetti introduced Burne-Jones to Ruskin, Holman Hunt,
Madox Brown, Arthur Hughes and his circle of friends in the

Alcestis and the Lament

*Left: Alcestis design painted on a pair of tiles, 1861.
A series of designs for tiles illustrating the heroines
from Chaucer's 'Legend of Good Women' was
amongst the first commissions Burne-Jones received
from the firm Morris, Marshall, Faulkner and Co. It
was adapted for embroidery in 1864 and inspired
the painting 'Chaucer's Dream' of 1865. The tiles at
this date were often painted by the women folk — his
wife Georgiana, Lucy Faulkner or her sister.*

*'The Lament' a watercolour of 1866. At the time he
painted this picture Burne-Jones came closest to the
work of Albert Moore. Unlike Albert Moore though,
he never treated the arrangement of the figures
purely decoratively but always created an
atmosphere which was the real theme. This picture
impresses by its melancholy and the decorative
elements are subservient to it.*

late 1850s. Ruskin was immediately impressed by the young artist and his work and began buying from him and finding patrons for him. He encouraged and gave out advice in a way that was uniquely Ruskin's, once again trying to mould Burne-Jones as he had the earlier Pre-Raphaelites. As with the young Inchbold, he toured Italy with him setting him to copy Tintoretto (instead of the landscape as in the former's case).

Rossetti's influence, most strong until 1860, gradually declined after that date although it is unquestionably there until the 1870s. A new group of artists joined the Rossetti circle around 1862; these were the students from the ateliers in Paris—Whistler, George Du Maurier, Edward Poynter, Thomas Lamont and Thomas Armstrong. They infused a greater worldliness into the enclosed medieval ideas of Rossetti's friends, a concern for painting a picture and not for telling a story with paint. A greater breadth of theme and treatment entered the works of Burne-Jones and indeed his old master. Whistler's *Symphony in White No.1* was painted in 1862 and at the same time Burne-Jones was painting his *Flower of God* which he treated as a harmony in red, and his *Green Summer* which was a harmony in green. It is difficult to assess how the

Portrait of a girl c.1866, in red crayon. Once owned by Swinburne, this drawing is the most tonal that the artist ever produced. During the mid 1860s he made many textural drawings in which the form emerges almost miraculously out of the shadows. They show how rapidly he overcame his technical limitations and one can quite justly compare them with the work of Seurat and Odilon Redon, fifty years later.

ideas passed from one artist to another but no doubt conversation turned on such points as the content and role of a painting. What was emerging in painting was exactly similar to the changes occurring in the decorative arts. The Gothic Revival was giving way to different ideals.

In 1864 Burne-Jones began to exhibit at the Old Watercolour Society's exhibitions. He made his debut with a number of works which immediately brought him to the attention of a few students of the Royal Academy schools. Through this he became friends with Henry Holiday, Albert Moore, and Edward Clifford. Already he had made the acquaintance of Simeon Solomon, William de Morgan and Spencer Stanhope. Thus a new generation of artists developed which was to become a progressive and dominant group for the next twenty years.

'THE EARTHLY PARADISE'

The verse that Morris wrote while he was at Oxford predictably demonstrated his preoccupation with medieval themes and language. Like the drawings his friend was making, it shows the influence of Fouqué, Charlotte M. Yonge and Walter Scott. A similar change occurred in his poetry as in the work of Burne-Jones in the early 1860s. The intense almost claustrophobic atmosphere gave way to a relaxed narrative style which was concerned with the effects of metre, architecture of form, and poetry as a conscious art work. Almost from the beginning Morris had planned to produce his *Earthly Paradise* poem in the form of an elaborately illustrated book and, of course, Burne-Jones was to have been the designer involved. The artist put much effort into the project and numerous designs were made. He consulted books of the fifteenth century, especially the *Hypnerotomachia Poliphili* (1499). Morris drew upon classical and medieval sources for his text and the *Hypnerotomachia* has a similar fusion. By this time (1864-5) Burne-Jones was looking to Mantegna for guidance in his work, who also was immensely nostalgic for the classical times, and so the project was central to his development as an artist.

For all their ambition, the book proved too complex and the text finally appeared in 1868 unadorned. However it had had a fundamental influence upon Burne-Jones. In all, he had made approximately a hundred designs which he drew upon for the rest of his life. *Zephyrus and Psyche* (1865), *Cupid Delivering*

Psyche (three versions 1865, 1867 and c.1870), *Cupid's First Sight of Psyche* (two versions 1867), *The Court of Venus* (c.1868), *Venus* (c.1872), *The Altar of Hymen* (1874), *The Mirror of Venus* (two versions 1867-77, 1873-7), *Pan and Psyche* (two versions 1869-74), *Pygmalion and the Image* (two series of four pictures 1869-71, 1868-79), *The Marriage of Psyche* (1875-1895), two large schemes of murals *The Cupid and Psyche Story* and *The Perseus Series* and many unfinished pictures all had their origin in the *Earthly Paradise* project.

In addition, an idea arose out of the book, of a group of pictures which together tell a story. This method enabled Burne-Jones to make reference to the classical legends without overburdening a single picture with storytelling. He isolated an archetypal incident in each one, which allowed him to concentrate on the pictorial qualities while still relating a narrative. *The Pygmalion Series* is a perfect example.

Allied to this is the role of mural painting as Burne-Jones interpreted it. As mentioned earlier, both his important examples came out of the *Earthly Paradise* illustrations. Unity was given to the individual pictures by the narrative, but each episode was simplified into a single action. The first set in the dining room of 1, Palace Green, Kensington was relatively clumsy but in the second series, begun in 1875, he reduced the accessory details to a minimum and concerned himself with decorative considerations. Thus *The Perseus Series* is the artist's best contribution to the art but it was never finished and it never fully covered the walls of 10, Carlton Gardens, London, for which it was intended. As he was technically unable to paint directly on to a wall surface, both series were conceived in terms of easel pictures, which is a definite weakness.

THE GRANGE

When Morris built his house in Bexley there had been provision in the plans for an additional house to enclose a central quadrangle. There a type of commune was to have developed. Burne-Jones and his wife were to have joined Morris and others would have followed, either staying there permanently or just attending a workshop. The concept was inherited both from the original Pre-Raphaelite brotherhood and from the Oxford plan to form a celibate colony in London. Until 1864 the idea persisted but it had finally to be given up

'The Grange' by T.M. Rooke 1897-1900. Burne-Jones moved into The Grange at Fulham in 1867 after giving up the idea of living with Morris at the Red House. He lived there until his death in 1898 but never owned it, unsuccessfully attempting to buy it in later life. A large garden studio was built to house his many large canvases and was, for a short time at the turn of the century, open to the public: many unfinished works were exhibited. The house has been pulled down in recent years to make way for tower blocks; what an ideal place it would have been for a Burne-Jones art gallery!

that year as the Burne-Jones family realised they could not afford such a drain on their pocket. Du Maurier writes on Christmas Day, 1864: 'Jones poor fellow has given up all idea of building his house; . . . He's looking for a house in Kensington and Poynter is going to take his rooms . . .'

After his marriage to Georgiana Macdonald in 1860, Burne-Jones moved to Russell Place; just before the birth of their son, Philip, the couple moved to 62 Great Russell Street. Another move followed in 1865, to Kensington Square. After

Georgiana Burne-Jones by Charles Fairfax Murray, 1870. Georgiana met her husband through his friendship with her brother, who also attended King Edward's School, Birmingham. Her book on her husband is a touching eulogy to his memory, filled with both information and insight. Murray became an assistant to Burne-Jones in 1866; like him he was a convinced Italophile and eventually lived in Florence, where he gathered together an important collection of early Italian paintings.

two years at this address their financial situation improved and they felt in need of a larger and more permanent home as by now their second child Margaret had arrived. It was found in the form of The Grange, North End Lane, Fulham. At that time Fulham was almost in the country. The house had been occupied by Samuel Richardson, the novelist, in the eighteenth century, and Burne-Jones was impressed by its atmosphere. A high wall enclosed the garden, which contained an orchard and a lawn with a large mulberry tree in the centre. Because of the relatively high rent and rates they took a joint tenancy with Wilfred Heeley, a friend from university days. This was to be their home for the rest of their lives. When they had moved in, a house warming party was given which was described by Madox Brown: '...Jones having moved into his new house, gave a dance, a very swell affair; the house being newly decorated in the 'Firm' taste looked charming, the women looked lovely. . .' Philip Webb designed furniture, the old painted cabinets remained from early days, wall hangings embroidered by 'Georgie' and Morris's wallpapers were all used to beautify the house.

Fame and repute

PATRONAGE
A new type of patron came into existence in the nineteenth century. He was middle class and had made his wealth from industry. He was generally a self-made man with nothing of the classical background of his eighteenth-century counterpart. These industrialists required an art that was easily assimilated and made reference to nature directly. William Mulready had found such a patron in John Sheepshanks in the 1820s, the Pre-Raphaelites found them in William Miller of Liverpool, T. E. Plint of Leeds, William Leathart of Newcastle, W. H. Trist of Brighton, and George Rae of Birkenhead. Rossetti passed on Plint and Leathart to Burne-Jones during his period of encouragement. Gradually over the next decade he began to build up a band of admirers who were eager to purchase his works. By 1867, as we have seen, he was able to move into larger premises.

Frederick Leyland, a wealthy Liverpool shipowner who was also a patron of Rossetti, William Graham, M.P. for Glasgow, and William Hamilton were enthusiastic buyers who first became interested in Burne-Jones's art when they saw it at the Old Watercolour Society's Exhibition in 1865. From the first, patrons and painter were on intimate terms, and at times the patrons played almost a creative part in the formation of a particular work. Burne-Jones deliberately sought their advice, either on aspects not immediately concerned with the paintings such as the suitability of the subject and its possible commercial value or on business matters that arose out of his dealings. Their enthusiasm led them into situations that almost became high farce; such was their impatience to outdo a rival for a painting that they would advance large sums. Burne-Jones then frequently became in arrears with a number of commissions at the same time. William Graham's passion for his friend's painting can be understood from a letter he wrote to him in 1869:

'I want to have *Love is Passing* very much and I am to have the little jew boy—you showed me yesterday—then the *Spring* and *Venus Mirror* and the sleeping princess's knights enchanted. And a fellow to the *Pygmalion* I saw yesterday,and the *Psyche and Pan* and if your busy brain produces something more beautiful than any of them *I am to have it*—is this not right,'

This type of interest was shown in the artist's work right through to his death in 1898. There was relatively little necessity for him to exhibit at public institutions apart from the prestige. After his unfortunate experience at the Old Watercolour Society (see page 25) he did not exhibit, with one exception, any major work from 1870 to the opening of the Grosvenor Gallery in 1877. That he was not displeased with this position is shown by a recollection of the period. 'Upon that followed the seven blissfullest years of work that I ever had; no fuss, no publicity, no teasing about exhibiting, no getting pictures done against time.' With Burne-Jones, painting was not a career but an integral part of the process of living; his paintings are always intimate autobiographical reflections and, logically, he was embarrassed by the institutional aspects of established art. It was inevitable that he demanded a personal contact with those people who wished to own his paintings.

The artist continued in middle life to infuse his relationships with comedy, frequently of the schoolboy kind, and the following story illustrates this. Two Italian models, a particularly beautiful man and woman, had just finished sitting for the melancholy lovers in *Love Among the Ruins;* '. . .while Gaetano (the man) was preparing to depart, she (the other model) pressed him to accept a cigar which she said Burne-Jones, who had been called out of the room, had purposely left upon the table for him. Whether she was actually in the plot or not did not subsequently transpire. but she was disappointed when he did not light it. Gaetano, however, did not care much about cigars, so on his way home, hearing some youths complain that they had no cigarettes, he impulsively presented them with Burne-Jones's cigar. He had not gone very far before he heard an explosion and a great cracking noise mingled with shrill imprecations hurled after his retreating form. The cigar was a sham one, full of fireworks, which had exploded at the first touch of a match' (from *The Richmond Papers* by A. M. W. Stirling).

Burne-Jones was untypical of English artists in the intimacy he had with his models. The story shows how he treated them as part of his circle of friends and not as studio props.

SCANDAL AT THE OLD WATERCOLOUR SOCIETY

Hesperus, Love Disguised as Reason, Night, Beatrice and *Phyllis and Demophoon* were sent to be exhibited at the Old Watercolour Society's Summer Exhibition in 1870. An anonymous letter arrived at the society objecting to the nudity of Demophoon. Quick to respond to accusations of indecency, the Society approached the artist asking him to withdraw the offending picture. Burne-Jones courteously agreed but the society made a subsequent act of great tactlessness. They asked Burne-Jones to choose a painting by Mr Carl Haag to go in its place. This was a most stupid proposition both in the choice of painter and in asking Burne-Jones to choose. (The press had already generated some ill feeling between the two artists by making absurd comparisons and drawing conclusions in favour of Haag.) Of course Burne-Jones refused to make any such selection. After the exhibition was over he sent in his resignation.

'Gentlemen, I have waited until the close of the exhibition before sending in a formal resignation of my position as Member of the Old Watercolour Society, but it can be no matter of surprise for you to receive it now. The conviction that my work is antagonistic to yours has grown in my mind for some years past, and cannot only have been felt on my side—therefore I accept your desertion of me this year merely as the result of so complete a want of sympathy between us in matters of Art, that it is useless for my name to be enrolled amongst yours any longer.'

In disgust at his treatment by the society his friend Frederick Burton also resigned.

MARIA ZAMBACCO

For many years there was a close connection between the Pre-Raphaelites and the Greek colony in London. Rossetti had begun the association in the 1850s and beautiful girls had posed for him, especially the Spartali sisters. Alexander Ionodes, a wealthy businessman, assembled a large collection of their work. Mrs Cassaveti, a patron of Burne-Jones, had a beautiful married daughter, Maria Zambacco, who modelled for him in the late 1860s. Their relation became much more than artist and model and for three years Burne-Jones was infatuated with her. During that time, 1869-71, he immortalised her magnificent features in picture upon picture; she appears as Venus in *Venus Epithalamia*, as Beatrice in *Beatrice*, as Phyllis in *Phyllis and Demophoon*, as Summer in a set of four *Seasons* and as the figure of Temperance in *Temperantia*. It is interesting to compare these voluptuous roles with those in which the features of Georgiana appear—*Charity* surrounded by children and *Spring* (not actually Georgiana but a similar type).

A whole series of drawings made of Maria's face claims to be the most perfect example of his art; his pencil became transfigured when she was before him. Her image is delicately feminine yet as enchanting and bewitching as a siren or Morgan le Fay. For a while he lost sight of the Holy Grail and switched Sir Galahad's role for Sir Lancelot's. When he finally became disillusioned with the affair he found it more difficult to disentangle himself from the enchantress than he wished. A letter from Rossetti to Madox Brown shows how turbulent the affair was. 'Poor old Ned's affairs have come to a smash together, and he and Topsy, after the most dreadful to do, started for Rome suddenly, leaving the Greek damsel beating up the quarters of all his friends for him and howling like Cassandra.'

It may well be for this reason that a nervous tension invades the work of the early 1870s, most noticeable in the first version of the *Briar Rose* series. But there were other reasons for the depression that he had during these years. He had begun to lose direction. Rossetti had at first given him complete confidence when he first joined him, then Watts had encouraged him and he systematically constructed a technique during the 1860s evolving a small scale art form that was intimate in tone. However, a new Italianate force began to motivate his pictures from 1865 and his canvases grew in size. Contact with Watts influenced both this and the subject matter (he in turn influenced Watts's *Psyche* and *Love and Life*). Large allegorical themes occupied him—*Love Praying to Mercury, The Evening Star, Luna, The Wheel of Fortune,* etc. However, Burne-Jones

'Maria', pencil, 1871. *During* his infatuation with
Maria, innumerable portraits were made of her.
They are without exception the most intensely felt
drawings Burne-Jones ever made and they always
suggest a timeless silence and a mood of sincerity
and sadness, as though the artist realised that her
beauty was subject to the ravages of time and their
relationship would inevitably come to an end.

'Temperantia' a watercolour, Burne-Jones's most
successful allegory; the model was Maria Zambacco.

never became involved in Watts's idea of preaching.

Consequent to these new interests Burne-Jones visited Italy in 1871 and 1873 and toured it, studying the works of Leonardo, Michelangelo, Andrea del Sarto, Luini, Botticelli, Mantegna, and Signorelli, as well as the interests of his former years—Giotto, Piero della Francesca, Uccello and Orcagna. From now on it was the artists of the High Renaissance that he investigated.

QUARREL WITH RUSKIN

Friendship with Ruskin could be a mixed affair. On one hand there was his generosity and his indefatigable interest in his friends' activity; but on the other he tended to expect all to follow his ideas and worship his gods. He showered his young friend with advice not always in sympathy with Burne-Jones's ideas. In 1870 Ruskin delivered a lecture on Michelangelo attacking him, '(Michelangelo) attempts to execute things beyond his power, had neither skill to lay a single touch of good oil painting nor patience to overcome even its elementary difficulties. .' What sort of impression was this likely to make upon a passionate admirer of the artist? Inevitably it led to a cooling between critic and painter. 'He read it to me just after he had written it, and as I went home I wanted to drown myself in the Surrey canal or get drunk. in a tavern—it didn't seem worthwhile to strive any more if he could think and write it.' Ever after it was only sentimental ties that kept them in contact with one another.

THE STUDIO IN THE 1870s

Refreshed from his bathe in the invigorating waters of Italian art Burne-Jones returned to his studio to confront a mass of unfinished work. Now he was able to tackle his old canvases and begin new projects.

One of the reasons for his incredible fecundity was his practice of employing a body of studio assistants to carry out the work that required little or no inventive power—transferring designs from drawing to canvas, making cartoons for decorative work, and executing decorative schemes. Charles Fairfax Murray took the first assistant's post in November 1866. At that time he was in effect a copyist making second versions, since the scale did not demand large studio activities. Thomas

George Howard made these three sketches whilst Burne-Jones was staying with him at Naworth Castle in Cumberland. Howard was an intimate friend of the artist and Morris as well as of many others of the group; he commissioned numerous items from the Firm and owned many of Burne-Jones's paintings including the important 'Annunciation' (now in the Lady Lever Art Gallery) and the 'Cupid and Psyche' frieze which was painted specially for his dining room at 1 Palace Green, Kensington. Howard himself was a capable landscape artist and a pupil of Giovanni Costa and Alphonse Legros.

Matthew Rooke first applied to William Morris for a post in the workshop but was passed on to Burne-Jones who took him as an assistant. He remained there until Burne-Jones's death, acting as chief assistant. Subsequently, John M. Strudwick, a successful painter in his own right, Francis Lathrop, an American decorative artist, Matthew Webb, another decorative artist, Gaetano Aeo, model turned artist, 'Chick' Harvey, the son of Burne-Jones's doctor, and Albert Jones, T. M. Rooke's brother-in-law, all worked at some time in the studio. Walter Crane worked on the murals in 1, Palace Green, Kensington, following Burne-Jones's small watercolour designs. Copies that deceived even the artist himself were made by Edward Clifford of early works like *Green Summer* 1864 and *An Idyll* 1861.

Obviously no artist could employ all these men for years at a time and they were circulated from one studio to another. The circuit to which Burne-Jones belonged included Henry Holiday, Spencer Stanhope, Watts and Lord Leighton.

PAINTINGS OF THE MIDDLE PERIOD (1870-1875)

Each Sunday morning from the time of his move to Turnham Green in 1872, Morris spent at The Grange. He read his latest poetry which was chiefly his translation of Virgil's *Aeneid*.

'Troy Story', oil, 1870-73. A most puzzling and ambiguous work, 'Troy' is a painting of a painting. Like a Mantegna polyptych in form, it symbolises the redirection of painting in the early 1870s for it treats a pagan theme – the fall of Troy – in a highly religious (traditionally Christian) way, representing the shift from the Gothic revival. The picture was never finished and as it stands today it is mostly the work of assistants.

'Laus Veneris', oil, 1872-5. Quite the most colourful painting by Burne-Jones, this represents the end of his early direction, for it sums up his concern with colour and texture. The picture is based upon a watercolour made in 1861 and the 'passing of Venus' in the background is also a reworking of a design for tiles of that year. The chair upon which the queen is seated is similar to one designed by Rossetti for the firm in 1861. Swinburne wrote a poem of the same title and on the same theme in the early 1860s but, typically, is more directly sensual.

Together he and Burne-Jones evolved the plan of a superbly illuminated manuscript copy with illustrations by the artist and decorations by Morris. As with the *Earthly Paradise* scheme, in the end it came to nothing but a few magnificent drawings. However, it prompted a large and complex painting entitled *The Story of Troy* in the form of a Renaissance polyptych. It is an intriguing picture, a painting of a painting in a frame, full of invention, ambitious, a secular altarpiece—symbolic of the new direction art had taken in the aesthetic movement.

The period produced great works—*The Sirens, The Golden Stairs, Love Among the Ruins, The Days of Creation*, etc., but the masterpieces were *Laus Veneris* and *The Beguiling of Merlin*. They exhibit his concerns with the picture as a rich surface, his serpentine line, fleshly Michelangelesque figures and intense psychological mood. Two-dimensionality is given emphasis to create an artificial world which is a concentration of the natural world much as the mind conceives it. The curvilinear features are climactial in *The Beguiling of Merlin*; one feels that the painting consists of one intricately coiled line and that if one pulled at a thread the whole would unravel like some ancient tapestry.

Other works were made during this period but, unlike these paintings, they are re-creations of designs from other media.

WORK FOR THE COMPANY

The new influences were operating in the designs for stained glass; the curving line finds superlative expression in the windows at Meole Brace (Shadrach, Meshach and Abednigo), 1870, Knotty Ash, Liverpool (Absolom) and Waterford, Herts (Miriam), both 1872. A monumental window of 1874 demonstrates his competence at handling large-scale projects. The east window at Easthampstead, Berkshire, shows an interesting mixture of references, to Fra Angelico, Mantegna, Signorelli and, of course, Michelangelo in the sybilline angels of judgement. Morris's contribution shows a tremendous advance; the colour—red, white and blue—is most effective, his star-studded ground creates an ingenious impression of the heavens opened. The distribution of the patterns created through the leading is a major innovation and was years ahead of its time.

After the re-organisation of the firm in 1875, Burne-Jones became the only designer of stained glass until the 1890s. But for this, his income would have been considerably smaller. Stained glass was not the only product of the firm that he played a large part in designing. A commission was received from Sir Lowthian Bell for a needlework tapestry to decorate his dining room at Rounton Grange, which had been erected from Philip Webb's plans. The theme was taken from Chaucer's *Romaunt of the Rose*; Burne-Jones made the designs and Morris prepared the working drawings. It was finished in 1880, the embroideresses being Sir Lowthian's wife and daughter.

Opposite: 'The Last Judgement', east window at St. Michael and St. Mary Magdalen's Church, Easthampstead, 1874. This was the most elaborate design made up to that date; there are numerous references to Italian masters such as Fra Angelico and Mantegna in its form but it is, nonetheless, a success. He has effectively made sense of a complex area of window space by relating each part to a whole and by making no attempt at perspective.

*'The Arming of Perseus', gouache, 1875. A.J. Balfour, who was later Prime
Minister, commissioned a scheme of decoration for his music room,
allowing Burne-Jones to choose the subject. Like George Howard's series,
he took the designs from his unpublished illustrations to Morris's 'Earthly
Paradise' made in the mid 1860s. The scheme took many years and in fact
was never fully realised. The series of which this is a part are full-scale
preparatory designs; the ten oil paintings that made up the final set are
now in Stuttgart Art Gallery.*

The established master

THE GROSVENOR GALLERY

Since its foundation in 1768 the Royal Academy had established itself as the mouthpiece for British painting. Foreigners looked to it to gain an impression of the activity in the field and, in having its schools, it also modelled the pattern of practising art of the future. Members formed a selection committee each year to decide what exhibits should be hung in the summer shows which inevitably reflected their conservative taste. Little room was given either to young artists or those who deviated from the straight and narrow path of the selectors' ideal. For generations young artists tried to secede; even the staid W.P. Frith had as a young man been a member of a group of secessionists, 'The Clique'. The Pre-Raphaelites were the most successful but suffered from having no exhibition area. They formed the Hogarth Club in 1858 for this purpose but it was to close in 1861. 1865 saw the opening of the Dudley Gallery which 'while exclusively devoted to drawings as distinguished from oil paintings should not in its use by exhibitors involve membership of a society'. It was open to all comers, amateur and professional alike, but a committee kept out the cranks. The gallery became a focal point for the group round Burne-Jones–Henry Holiday, Edward Poynter, Simeon Solomon, Walter Crane, Spencer Stanhope, William de Morgan, Albert Moore, Edward Clifford, and many of the Pre-Raphaelite circle. Oil paintings were included in 1870 and Burne-Jones sent four small panels in 1871, and *Love Among the Ruins*, and *The Hesperides* in 1873.

A group of artists, the followers of Burne-Jones and the Pre-Raphaelites, were rapidly diverging from the establishment painters and felt the need of their own exhibition room. They had become established as the fashionable painters of the 1870s, and, together with the decorative artists, they comprised

Above and opposite: two self caricatures of the artist attempting to unite his body with the fantasy of his mind. In these drawings Burne-Jones humourously states his dilemma, that of reconciling his intense vision with the banalaties of everyday life. Typically, these revelatory sketches were sent to amuse a young friend of his, Katie Lewis; in an unguarded moment he has allowed us to enter his innermost mind.

the 'Aesthetic Movement' which was bringing the discoveries of the previous decade to the notice of society at large. In 1877 they found such a room in the form of the Grosvenor Gallery off Bond Street. It was an Italianate building designed by an architect named Sams. The money needed for the project was supplied by Sir Coutts Lindsay, himself an amateur artist of some ability. Charles Halle, a painter, and Phillip Comyns Carr, an author and critic, organised the exhibitions.

Taste was the keyword; the interior was furnished with gilt Italian chairs and the walls were lined with red velvet. Each picture was allowed ample hanging space, unlike the cramming at the Royal Academy. Exhibition was by invitation and in fact the gallery was very exclusive and was in reality restricted to Burne-Jones and his followers—George Howard, a remarkable painter who became 9th Earl of Carlisle, Alphonse Legros, Giovanni Costa, G. H. Mason, Matthew Ridley Corbet, Thomas Armstrong, Whistler, Albert Moore, Walter Crane, Lord Leighton and Alma-Tadema.

Much was said of the gallery not being in opposition to the Royal Academy and a lot of importance was given to the fact that Millais and Leighton were exhibitors, but this did. not

basically alter the position. It was a secessionist gallery, it did offer a threat to the domination of the Royal Academy and there is no doubt that opposition to that august body was created. The Grosvenor Gallery was the showplace of the Aesthetes, it gave them an opportunity to display their culture and quality of civilisation. Recitals were given there which reached their zenith when the Abbé Liszt performed there in 1882.

But all was not well. Burne-Jones disliked intensely the decor, which he believed clashed with his paintings, and Ruskin was incensed by its rivalry with the Academy. He too hated the red plush but even more he hated Whistler's paintings; his slanderous attack on his *Harmony in Blue and Gold—The Falling Rocket* brought about the famous Ruskin *v* Whistler trial.

Burne-Jones sent *The Beguiling of Merlin, The Days of Creation, Mirror of Venus, Spes, Fides, Temperantia, St. George* and *A Sibyl* to the opening show. He was an instant success and found himself sought after as a portrait painter, a position in which he was not at his best. Nonetheless, he made some remarkable examples; he did not seek for a likeness but made time stand still for the sitter and let their faces express a calm, trance-like dignity as though he saw into the depth of their being.

Success at the Grosvenor gave him access to the highest social circles. Already his admirers included the Balfours, the Grahams

and the Hamiltons; now he added the Wyndhams, the
Gladstones, the Lewises and the Leighton-Warrens. Other
spectacular figures came and went from his studio—Sir Henry
Irving, Ellen Terry, Oscar Wilde, Paderewski, Cosima Wagner,
Sarah Bernhardt, Aubrey Beardsley, Arthur Sullivan and many
others. They admired his gentle wit, his learning, his ability to
bring to life the magic of ancient legends. Children loved him
because they felt special when he talked to them. He was
intensely nostalgic for his own youth and would parody his age
for them each time his own birthday came round. Unlike many
of his contemporaries he never took himself completely
seriously; always, even in the most precious things, he was able
to see the vitality. The struggle he had in coming to terms with
reality and his desire to enter the world of his imagination are
touchingly satirised in the series of caricatures he sent to a small
girl, Katie Lewis.

A studio was built in the garden at The Grange to house the
many canvases that he was working on, to give more light and
to encompass the larger paintings. In it a piano was installed and
many impromptu recitals were given by his friends. Wagner was
a favourite composer but Burne-Jones was not wholly converted
to the earlier operas; *Parsival* he loved above all. When
Paderewski visited the studio he sat for a pencil portrait and
Burne-Jones used the features in his questing knights in the
Morte d'Arthur tapestries.

ROTTINGDEAN

Life as a popular painter could be something of a strain for
an artist with a delicate constitution. For this reason, in 1881
Burne-Jones bought a house on the edge of the Sussex downs at
Rottingdean. Here he escaped the pressures of the metropolis
and relaxed a while. His friend and architect 'Willie' Benson
adapted the building, combining two small houses and creating
a studio. At the back, one of the rooms was furnished as a
tavern and called 'The Merry Mermaid'. Many friends enjoyed
relaxing and the jovial company at the house by the sea.
Proximity to the sea inspired a series of mermaid subjects
culminating in *The Depths of the Sea* (1886), the only picture
he exhibited at the Royal Academy. It was an unusually sinister
subject, at least that is how people interpreted it, but in fact it
is precisely the same in theme as *The Beguiling of Merlin*

(1870-76): a seductress carries off her prey to his doom – the bottom of the sea in the former and encased in a tree in the latter.

For a time the large *Arthur in Avalon* was worked on at Rottingdean but, on the whole, only small intimate items engaged his attention. He began the practice of using gold and silver paint alone and he started the series of watercolours on the names of flowers that were to be published posthumously as *The Flower Book*.

THE ROME MOSAICS

Throughout the nineteenth century British artists were unanimous in their desire for a national school of mural decoration. Traditionalist and innovator alike joined in the call. Benjamen Haydon initiated the scheme to decorate the new Houses of Parliament in the 1840s, but nothing came of it after the competition and in spite of Maclise, Watts, Dyce and Madox

North End House, Rottingdean, became Burne-Jones's other home when he purchased it in 1881. His friend W.S. Benson, who was an architect, adapted the property, joining two houses and creating a studio. It was used after periods of intense work to allow the artist to relax and entertain his friends. As it stands today there is little to recall his period of ownership except a single window designed by Morris and some paintings of a comic nature Burne-Jones made to amuse grandchildren. Across the green stands the church with a superb set of windows commemorating the marriage of his daughter to J.W. Mackail. In the churchyard a plaque commemorates the fact that the artist's ashes were scattered there in 1898.

*'The Tree of Life', a gouache of a design used in the scheme of mosaics
decorating the apse of St. Paul's American Church in Rome. The
architect, G.E. Street died before the mosaics were anything like complete
and, in fact, they fell short of Burne-Jones's requirements. In the above
design, Burne-Jones has stressed the symbolic triumph of the cross,
eliminating the gory aspects. The very proto-Art Nouveau tree upon which
he hangs symbolically encompasses Adam and Eve thus forgiving them for
their fall. At each side are references to other parts of the story, the corn
to the Eucharist and the lily to the annunciation.*

Brown no unified school developed. Burne-Jones was equally
obsessed, 'I want big things to do and vast spaces, and for
common people to see them and say Oh!—only Oh!'

His opportunity came in 1882. The American Protestant
colony in Rome wished to build a church; it commissioned G.
E. Street to design it. It wanted to make the church special and,
aware of the traditions of Rome, it asked for an elaborate
scheme of decoration for its interior. Street teamed up with
Burne-Jones who designed a mosaic for the apse and chancel
arches.

The theme chosen was Christ in majesty attended by the four
archangels situated above saints, angels and martyrs. Above the
chancel arches were scenes of a bloodless crucifixion, the Tree
of Life and a nativity (later this was changed and an
annunciation was substituted). The tesserae were supplied by

the firm who executed it, the Venezia–Murano Co., and Morris helped select the colour scheme.

There were many hitches, and what started as a most promising project soon turned sour. T. M. Rooke happened to be in Rome and when called upon to intervene for Burne-Jones found it impossible to make the company follow his instructions. Burne-Jones became finally disillusioned when the money ran out. After a few attempts to take it up again it remained unfinished at his death. In 1904 Rooke was approached by the church and completed the scheme. However good his intentions, his contribution gives an impression of clumsiness and the mural falls short of the magnificence Burne-Jones had intended.

THE LATE PAINTINGS

Absolute mastery of his medium came to Burne-Jones in his final period. His techniques attained a virtuosity that had rarely been reached before; he was, like a magician, able to create marvels with limited means. Nothing was superfluous, each line or shading was essential to a drawing. Like the mannerists before him he took liberties with anatomy to create the maximum of expression. Long elegant nymphs are created in gold and silver, subtleties of mood are suggested, nuances of poise and facial expression. Sensitivity to texture, always a feature of his work, reached its highest manifestation in his last paintings.

The late paintings are more pictorial and less intense than

Head study for 'The Hours', pencil, c.1878. First conceived in the early 1860s, 'The Hours' was finished in the oil version in 1883, a differing water-colour may have been completed in about 1865.

41

those of earlier years. The time he spent as a designer of stained glass shows in the decorative role of the pictures; every inch is important in its relationship to the whole.

Three works show the artist at the height of his powers, *The Briar Rose* series of four paintings, *The Marriage of Psyche* and *Arthur in Avalon*. *The Briar Rose* and *The Marriage* pictures are all reworkings of earlier designs but *Arthur in Avalon* was completely original and is, without question, his greatest work. It took on a symbolic role for him; he identified with the sleeping king and even adopted his pose when he himself slept. Begun in 1881, he worked on it for seventeen years, attending to it on the day before he died. It can be taken as an autobiographical painting; Burne-Jones creates a mood of passivity, the riot of living is stilled, quietly the artist withdraws into his inner world. Attendant queens wait and watch for an event which will cause the king to awake and summon his strength to save the world—such is the power of art. Above all the picture is about silence. The artist calls for us to stop our industry and be still; he has created a mood of tranquillity. In order to do this he deliberately chose an immense scale to work in; the onlooker is thus dwarfed into submission and enters the painting as though it were a building. The only medium which equals this impact is the cinema which it so obviously anticipates.

KING ARTHUR

On Saturday 12th January 1895 at the Lyceum Theatre, London, Sir Henry Irving appeared in a new play by Phillip Comyns Carr entitled *King Arthur*. Incidental music was composed by Sir Arthur Sullivan and costumes and sets were designed by Burne-Jones. Like the Rome mosaics the play presented an opportunity for him to fulfil a fundamental desire, he could almost literally enter one of his paintings and become absorbed into the legend. As with the mosaics, however, it fell far short of his ideal.

'The armour is good—they have taken pains with it—made in Paris and well understood—I wish we were not barbarians here. The dresses were well enough if the actors had known how to wear them—one scene I made very pretty—of the wood in Maytime—that has gone to nothing—fir trees which I hate instead of beeches and birches which I love—why?—never mind.'

Top left: 'A dinner party', watercolour, c.1890. A loathing for certain nouveau riche ostentation and vulgarity stimulated a whole series of biting caricatures from Burne-Jones.

Above: portrait of Helen Mary Gaskel, pencil, 1898. An ardent admirer and intimate of the artist, Mrs Gaskel had the privilege of being asked advice on certain late works. Through her intercession the foreground of 'Arthur in Avalon' is massed with flowers instead of rocks.

Left: Fredereck Leyland's tomb (designed 1894). It is not generally realised that Burne-Jones designed three-dimensional objects; in fact he made quite a few designs, but this tomb is unique in his oevre and was prompted by his affection for one of his greatest patrons.

How highly he thought of the story is shown in a letter of 1895. 'Lord! How that Sangraal story is ever in my mind and thoughts continually—was ever anything in the world beautiful as that is beautiful? If I might. . . dedicate the last days to that tale?'

That, in effect, is what he did. In the work of his final eight years he was occupied with his masterpiece *Arthur in Avalon, The Failure of Sir Launcelot,* a huge set of tapestries depicting the departure of the knights, and illustrations for the Kelmscott Press books on the subject as well as the play.

THE KELMSCOTT PRESS

Founded in 1891, the Press was a fulfilment of Morris's and his friend's lifetime of interest in book design. It began in Oxford with the magazine, continued in the *Earthly Paradise,* and *Aeneid* schemes and reached a high point in Morris's illuminated manuscripts. In the Press books Morris designed the type and decorative settings and borders and Burne-Jones made the illustrations. Catterson-Smith prepared line designs from the artist's preliminary drawings which were engraved on to the block by Heaton-Hooper.

The collaboration produced some of the finest books since medieval times. In no way were they innovatory or functional; they were indeed very expensive. and only available to the wealthy connoisseur, but above all they were exceptionally beautiful. Chaucer was a lifelong interest to both men and the Kelmscott edition qualifies as their success. It contains 87 illustrations and was the pride of Burne-Jones. 'I am beside myself with delight over it. . .when the book is done. . .it will be like a pocket cathedral.'

Chaucer's stories enabled him to express his own themes through a process of selection, and as a result the book tells much about Burne-Jones. Many designs are variants on earlier pictures: *The Romaunt of the Rose* series are similar to the embroidery designs on the story, an illustration to *The Parliament of Fowls* makes an interesting comparison with *The Forge of Cupid* of 1861. The stories he selected to illustrate are close to those on which he had based existing pictures, for example 'The Clerk of Oxford's Tale' has much in common with *King Cophetua and the Beggar Maid* (1884) and *Love Among the Ruins* (1873, 1893) has a very Chaucerian theme.

STAINED GLASS

In the vast west window of St. Phillip's, Birmingham, is a mighty stained glass panel of the Last Judgement. As in the other media he used, Burne-Jones excels in his final period. The figures are massively conceived, two vast angels blow 'the last trump', as below earth crumbles into dust and the graves open. Above is a vision of Christ in majesty. The window space, typical of a classical building of this kind, is large and many a stained glass artist has failed to utilise the space offered on this dimension. Gothic architecture generally creates small pointed windows or a large window conveniently divided into smaller areas. Many designers in the earlier part of the century had capably come to terms with this situation but had been defeated by the churches of classical design. Burne-Jones's glass is conceived in terms of the architecture, it is monumental and its architectonic arrangement successfully relates it to the window space.

HONOURS

Death came to Burne-Jones on 17th June 1898. He was 65. *Arthur in Avalon* was left incomplete, yet so near to completion. There is a justice in it being unfinished; as we see

Sketch for 'Arthur in Avalon' from a Fred Hollyer photograph. Avalon was Burne-Jones's big obsession from 1881, when it was first concieved, until his death. The above sketch shows an early plan to include the warring knights at each side. At the same time, on either side there was to have been panels showing the hill fairies who were watching and waiting for the time when Arthur would be needed by the world. In its final form emphasis is made on the shrine with the body of the king with the attendant queens protecting his rest. Of epic proportions Avalon' is a masterpiece of late period; it now hangs in the art museum in Ponce, Puerto Rico, a tribute to their intelligence and the short-sightedness of the British museums who allowed it to be sold in the early 1950s.

the king sleeping we are made to remember the mortality of the artist. When he died he was internationally acclaimed, the French symbolist painters acknowledged a debt to him as did the Belgians and Austrians. His works had been exhibited in Paris from 1878 onwards, in 1889 he was made Chevalier of the Legion of Honour. Reluctantly he received a baronetcy in 1894, having received an honorary D.C.L. at Oxford in 1881. The New Gallery gave a memorial exhibition in the winter of 1898-9 which was followed by important exhibitions at The Burlington Fine Arts Club (1899), the Leicester Galleries (1904) and Manchester School of Art (1905).

BIBLIOGRAPHY
Memorials of Edward Burne-Jones; G.B-J. (Georgiana Burne-Jones); Macmillan, 1904.
Burne-Jones; Fortunée de Lisle; Methuen, 1904.
The Flower Book; Sir Edward Burne-Jones; The Fine Art Society, 1905.
Burne-Jones; J.E. Phythian; Grant Richards, 1908.
Sir Edward Burne-Jones; Malcolm Bell; Newnes Art Library, 1917.
Sir Edward Burne-Jones; Arsene Alexandre; Newnes Art Library (second series), 1917.
Letters to Katie; Ed. W. Graham Robertson; Macmillan, 1925.
Burne-Jones; Martin Harrison and William Waters; Barrie and Jenkins, 1973 (republished 1989).
Edward Burne-Jones; Penelope Fitzgerald; Michael Joseph, 1973.
Burne-Jones; Catalogue of the Arts Council Exhibition; John Christian, 1975.

MUSEUMS WHERE WORKS MAY BE SEEN
Birmingham Art Gallery; The Tate Gallery; The Victoria and Albert Museum; Fulham Library; National Museum of Wales, Cardiff; Carlisle Art Gallery; Lady Lever Art Gallery, Port Sunlight, Birkenhead; Fitzwilliam Museum, Cambridge; Ashmolean Museum, Oxford; Whitworth Art Gallery, Manchester; Manchester City Art Gallery; Bradford Art Gallery; Cecil Higgins Museum, Bedford; The Watts Gallery, Compton, Surrey; Glasgow Art Gallery.

THE PRINCIPAL EVENTS OF BURNE-JONES'S LIFE

1833   Edward Coley Burne Jones born on 28th August
1844   Burne-Jones goes to King Edward's School, Birmingham
1854   Burne-Jones meets Dante Gabriel Rossetti
1856   Burne-Jones and Morris produce a magazine
1857   Rossetti introduces Burne-Jones to the Prinseps
1858   Hogarth Club founded
1859   Burne-Jones visits Italy with Faulkner and Prinsep
1860   Marries Georgiana Macdonald. Windows for Oxford cathedral and Waltham Abbey
1861   Morris, Marshall, Faulkner and Co. founded. Burne-Jones visits Italy
1862   Whistler, Du Maurier and others join Rossetti's circle
1864   First exhibits at the Old Watercolour Society
1865   Move to Kensington Square. Dudley Gallery opened
1867   Move to Fulham. 'Cupid's First Sight of Psyche'
1868   Morris's 'The Earthly Paradise'
1869   Affair with Maria Zambacco (till 1871)
1870   Resigns from Old Watercolour Society. Meole Brace window. Ruskin's attack on Michelangelo
1871   Burne-Jones visits Italy
1872   Windows at Knotty Ash, Liverpool and Waterford, Herts
1873   Burne-Jones visits Italy
1874   Window at Easthampstead. 'The Altar of Hymen'
1875   Burne-Jones now The Firm's sole glass designer
1876   'The Beguiling of Merlin' completed
1877   Grosvenor Gallery opened. 'The Mirror of Venus'
1878   'Pan and Psyche'
1880   Completion of tapestry for Rounton Grange
1881   Buys house at Rottingdean. 'Arthur in Avalon' begun
1882   Commissioned to decorate church in Rome
1884   'King Cophetua and the Beggar Maid'
1886   'The Depths of the Sea' 1889
1889   Burne-Jones created Chevalier of the Legion of Honour
1891   Kelmscott Press founded
1893   'Love Among the Ruins'
1894   Burne-Jones created a baronet
1895   'King Arthur' opens at the Lyceum Theatre
1898   Sir Edward Burne-Jones dies on 17th June

INDEX
Page numbers in italic refer to illustrations